One Small Garden

One Small Garden

Barbara Nichol • Illustrated by Barry Moser

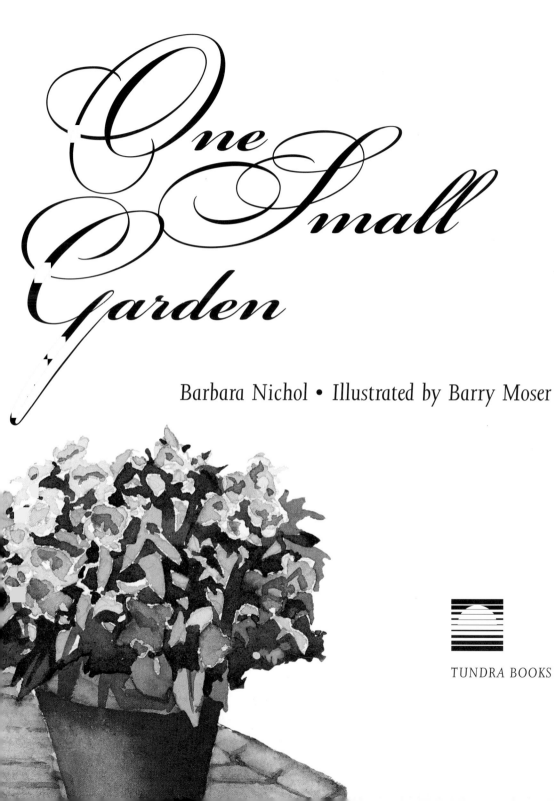

TUNDRA BOOKS

Published in Canada by Tundra Books,
481 University Avenue, Toronto, Ontario M5G 2E9

Published in the United States by Tundra Books of Northern New York,
P.O. Box 1030, Plattsburgh, New York 12901

Library of Congress Control Number: 00-135464

National Library of Canada Cataloguing in Publication Data

Nichol, Barbara (Barbara Susan Lang)
   One small garden

ISBN 0-88776-475-4

1. Gardens – Anecdotes – Juvenile literature. 2. Gardening – Juvenile literature.
3. Nichol, Barbara (Barbara Susan Lang) – Juvenile literature. I. Moser, Barry. II. Title.

SB457.N52 2001   j635   C00-932275-2

We acknowledge the support of the Canada Council for the Arts and the Ontario Arts
Council for our publishing program.

We acknowledge the financial support of the Government of Canada through the Book
Publishing Industry Development Program for our publishing activities.

Design: Barry Moser

Printed and bound in Belgium

1 2 3 4 5 6.   06 05 04 03 02 01

Table of Contents

FOR *DAVID COLE*
—B.N.

FOR MY DEAR FRIENDS JOHN & MEL EVANS
and to the glorious gardens & restorative repasts at Fox Hollow.
—B.M.

Acknowledgments

Barbara Nichol thanks John Conlan, Ross Anderson, Barbara Burkhardt, Al MacWilliams, Tess Steinkolk, David Walker, Jeffrey Pratt, John and Elizabeth Nichol, Graeme Gibson, Richard Prince, Marjorie Nichol, Sarah Milroy, Timothy Cole, and Jennifer Hollyer. For checking her facts, she thanks Nancy Dengler, professor of botony at the University of Toronto, and David Tarrant, *The Canadian Gardener*.

Thanks and love to Jessica and Sarah Eisen for their incorruptible vegan example; as always, to Benjamin Eisen and Lizzie, Jonathan, and Nellie Milroy, and to my goddaughter, Amy McQuaig.

Many thanks to Kathy Lowinger, whose idea it was to write a book about the garden.

To my dear readers:

In the heart of a city, downtown, there is a small garden.

The truth is, there are many gardens here — thousands of gardens — adjoining thousands of houses in this place that used to be a forest.

This garden, though, is hidden from the street. It's been here for a hundred years, nestled close beside a house — a house built long ago behind another house. This is a garden you would not suspect is there.

This garden — or little piece of land — it has a history, of course. It has a story — a story that's as ancient as the world. Most of it's a history we'll never know about. Most things that happen in the world are never written down. Most things that happen in the world take place when no one's looking.

Perhaps this little patch of ground had other buildings on it once: a little shed, perhaps — some little place of shelter. It might have been a farm. Perhaps there was an inn nearby. Perhaps a road went through, a road made out of logs to keep the carts from sinking.

Whatever thing this little piece of land has been — forest or pasture or homestead or road — there came a day when it was stitched into the huge patchwork of the city. There came a day when someone decided this piece of land would be a garden.

That is the role this patch of ground will play for now — a garden in a neighborhood called Cabbagetown. The garden's in a city that used to be Fort York, and then it was called York, and now is called Toronto. It's possible it will one day have another name, or just be known as somewhere where a city used to be.

I have visited this garden for the past ten years or so.

In this book are some of the things I've seen here, some of the things I've learned about the plants, some of the plants and animals that caught my eye and the stories that they brought to mind — stories I've been told. The stories in this book are little stories — parts of stories — the kinds of things that usually aren't written down.

As far as I know — from what I can remember, as far as I've been told — everything that's in this book is true.

— Barbara Nichol

One Small Garden

One

The Raccoon Family

TEN YEARS AGO, in the early morning, there would often be raccoons roaming the garden. This was at dawn, when most people are still asleep.

Raccoons go about their business at night. They leave their homes after dark and go out to accomplish the things they need to, to carry on their lives: to eat and to survive. Because, for the most part, we do these things by day, we don't often see raccoons. It's easy to forget they're all around us, living with us in the city, so nearby.

10

In the very early morning, though, the raccoons would sometimes dawdle in the gardens on their way home to sleep. They would stop on the roof of a garage next to the garden – a flat roof covered by a vine.

The vine still grows there and now covers the whole roof. It's a Virginia creeper. A Virginia creeper vine grows very large and comes out with blue-black berries in the fall.

The littlest raccoons would take their time in the Virginia creeper, picking through the leaves and berries. The grown raccoons would wait for the little ones to come along. When the young raccoons had caught up, the raccoon family would climb down the side of a tall tree at the corner of the garage, the big raccoons going first.

The little raccoons would grope about the trunk before beginning the climb down to the fence that led them home. They were nervous about climbing straight down. The grown raccoons would wait. It was a short climb down the tree – only about three feet – but straight down.

Then, in a slow line, the family would travel along the fence top: big and small, identical shapes in different sizes, round and peaceful, not knowing they were being watched, five or six raccoons in silhouette.

And then they would just seem to disappear. One moment they would be there on the fence and then they would be gone completely, disappearing in the leaves. It was impossible to catch the moment when they left the garden.

They seemed to vanish into the pink air.

A Line of Ants

TEN YEARS AGO there was a maple tree just inside the gate. The tree was very tall — as tall as a three- or four-story house. Its limbs reached up high and spread out over the garden. In the summer it sheltered the garden under green leaves. Maple leaves have a shape scientists call palmate, like the underside of someone's open hand. The maple leaf has five broad points for fingers.

One visitor to the garden called the maple tree the guardian of the garden. It seemed to protect the garden under its boughs.

If the tree hadn't been right beside the gate where people come and go, no one would have noticed the line of ants going about their business on the bark — hundreds of them, making their way around the base of the tree and up the trunk. They would disappear into the bark. They would disappear like the raccoons.

They always seemed to be there, orderly and busy, hard at work.

The store that sells young plants and tools for gardens is called a nursery, a word we use for rooms where human babies sleep. At the nursery they explained that the ants had made a home inside the tree. They said that this could harm the tree. They recommended a powder to be sprinkled in their path.

"This powder won't harm any other animals," they said, "because it isn't poisonous. It's deadly, though, to ants. The powder's made of sharp and tiny particles. The ants will touch the particles. They'll be scratched and injured and they'll die."

The Poisoned Gardener

This is a story about a boy who grew up in Vancouver.

WHEN RICHARD PRINCE was small, his next-door neighbor was a man who loved to tend his garden. Every evening after work — spring, summer, and fall — and all day long on weekends, the neighbor could be found behind his house, doing what one needs to, to have a handsome garden. He watered the plants, he pulled up the weeds, he added fertilizer to the soil. And he sprayed the plants with poisons. He did this to rid the garden of insects and diseases. He did this to rid the garden of pests.

In the neighbor's garden the poisons worked their magic. The apples on the apple tree were round and red and perfect; the grass, an even patch of emerald green. The bushes were not powdery with fungus. The roses bore no spots.

It was like a garden in a picture book — like a vision in a fairy tale — and so it stayed for years. It might still be perfect, although this is unlikely, things changing as they do. In any case, the story ended long ago.

The gardener never did grow old. Instead, he became pale and thin in middle age, and died of a disease the experts say comes from breathing in the sorts of poisons he'd been spraying in his garden. The gardener next door had rid the garden of pests. He'd sprayed to make the insects and diseases vanish. And then he vanished too.

Plants Use Poisons

GARDENERS USE POISONS to protect their plants, and plants use poisons too. Lilies of the valley are poisonous to eat. Daffodil bulbs are poisonous. Animals will leave them be.

And plants have other ways that they defend themselves. There are plants that protect themselves with bitter taste. These plants are safe as well, at least from being eaten.

There are plants that send out chemicals into the soil, so that other plants can't grow close by. Black walnut trees do this. They don't have to share their water, food, and space with other plants.

Roses protect themselves with thorns. Poison ivy protects itself

by delivering its famous itchy rash. There are evergreens that give off chemicals to keep other plants and maybe insects off as well. This explains the smell of Christmas trees.

Animals use such things as teeth and claws, horns and stingers. We protect ourselves with guns and gates and laws and lies, and by running away.

Two

Scissors

This happened about forty years ago.

TWO LITTLE GIRLS came up with a plan. They would cut down a tree with scissors. It seemed quite possible, like something in a cartoon. They chose a small tree in their backyard, hidden from the view of the house.

The girls set out after breakfast one Saturday to make a day of their task. They took their scissors – the sort of blunt scissors children are given to use. They took their lunch in paper bags, cold drinks, and Band-Aids for emergencies.

They settled in at the foot of the tree and got to work, scratching at the trunk. As soon as they had set about their task, it was obvious to the girls that they would fail. The tree was tougher than it looked. They were not going to be able to make so much as a nick in the bark of the tree. The scissors were as useless against the tree as they would have been against a sidewalk. The girls, wisely, gave up right away.

So this story ends here at the beginning. But the tree was as busy on the inside as the girls were at its bark. Just inside the bark are tiny tubes, like drinking straws, that carry water and nutrition up and down inside the trunk. To give you an idea of how industrious a maple tree can be, a big tree such as this can send a hundred pails of water from the roots into the leaves in just one day. The water lifts as vapor in the air.

Imagine this on summer days: water lifting up into the sky from all the trees, invisible and silent from the leaves.

The bark is what protects the tree from creatures such as little girls.

Leaves

PLANTS take minerals and water from underneath the ground, and send them to their leaves to make their food. Plants make food by using sunlight on their leaves. The food they make's a sort of sugar.

To make their food, plants do all they can to face the light. Their leaves are spaced along their branches so that, as much as possible, they will not block each other from the sun. Plants move and bend. They turn their leaves this way and that to catch the sun. A sunflower will turns its face throughout the day, following the sun above it in the sky. It turns its head as though it's watching. Sunflowers are very tall. They grow as tall as people.

Hollyhocks

HOLLYHOCKS are tall flowers too — taller than a child. They bloom on stalks, with flowers coming out not just at the top but down the stem as well.

Hollyhocks don't grow well in this garden.

16

There were some planted for a while. They came down with an illness known as "rust," a disease that is a tiny plant that makes a home of larger plants, robbing them of strength.

A couple of miles from the garden, across the middle of town, past gas stations and school yards and storefronts and intersections with honking horns and housing projects for the poor, is an old apartment building. It looks to be abandoned from outside. The windows are all boarded up. The lawn around the building is brown and dry in summer. No one tends this building or this lawn.

But no one needs to tend its hollyhocks. In the hot sun, across a peeling wall, there grows each year a hedge of hollyhocks — a stand of salmon-colored flowers, four or five feet high.

Some plants do well in hot dry soil. It seems that hollyhocks are one of these. From what we know, this flower comes from Palestine.

Gardeners do their best to give plants the conditions they're best suited for — the surroundings that they had where they first grew. Gardeners pay attention to how much water they provide; to what is in the soil. They offer plants bright sunshine or the shade of trees; do what they can for plants that need protection from the winter storms.

In Charge of the Lawn

WHEN JEFFREY PRATT was a boy, he took charge for a while of the family's lawn.

There's a lot of work that goes into a lawn. A lawn — clipped and green and flat — is not something that ever happens naturally. A lawn is a human invention made of grass, in the same way that a lightbulb's an invention made of glass and wire. We make our lawns from grass plants because grass leaves do not suffer when they're stepped on. Grass grows well in areas where people play and walk around.

But lawns require work. You have to water the lawn. You have to give it fertilizer. You have to pull out the weeds. You have to kill the pests that eat the grass. You have to mow the lawn – cut off the tiny grass leaves – not too short. You have to cut it often, once a week or so in seasons when it's growing.

Jeffrey Pratt did all these things. He thought about it all day long. When Jeffrey wasn't working on the lawn, he'd lie on his bed upstairs. From the top bunk he watched over the garden. He'd watch the lawn outside. When anything fell on the grass – a maple key, perhaps – he'd run downstairs and out the door to pick it up.

Grass has tiny flowers, almost too small to see. They open once a year, each flower for an hour or so.

Watering

THE BEST TIME to water the garden is in the morning.

If you sprinkle water during the heat of the day, much of it will evaporate before it lands. If you sprinkle when the sun is strong, the beads of water magnify the sun. The sun can burn the leaves. If you water after sundown, you'll leave the garden damp at night and court disease.

The best way to water is thoroughly – long enough so that the water soaks well down into the ground. If you water only briefly, the roots of plants will not grow down as deep. They won't need to travel down to find their water, and they won't.

Plants with shallow roots will suffer if water's ever scarce. They won't have roots down deep where, in a drought, there might be water left for them to find.

18

Three

THE TREE EXPERT • MULBERRY • ROOTS • BUTCH

The Tree Expert

THE ANT POWDER didn't stop the ants in the big maple tree. The rain washed it away. Finally, an expert came to see the maple near the gate. (Experts, by the way, are people who know more than most of what other experts in their field believe. They are sometimes right and sometimes wrong.)

The expert watched the ants. He watched their journey up and down the trunk. He was concerned to see them in such numbers.

He said that if a colony of ants is living in a tree, there must be rotten places in the trunk, hollow places for the ants to make a home. How large a home they'd found, it was impossible to know.

There are some trees that do just fine when ants are living in their bark. There are even trees, in other places in the world, with hollows in their trunks, especially to give a home to ants. The maple wasn't one of these.

An ants' nest, by the way, is like a city, but for ants. Or look at it another way: a city's like an ants' nest, but for people. A city's like a nest made out of streets and stores and such.

19

Mulberry

UNDERNEATH the maple is a mulberry, a tree that comes from Asia. Its shape is full of twists and turns. This mulberry is shorter than the maple, but it's older. The mulberry's a slower growing tree.

Every second summer the mulberry bears fruit; the berries look like raspberries but darker, soft and purple. When the fruit is ripe, it drops onto the lawn and paths. It drops into the bushes and the flower beds — everywhere its inky purple stains. The squirrels and birds make off with what they can.

There are gardeners who won't plant trees like this. They say fruit trees are messy. Many gardeners want nature to be tidy.

The maple and the mulberry have grown up close together; it looks at first as if the two are really one. Their roots would no doubt be entangled in the ground.

Sometimes the roots of different trees will join together underground. The water taken by the roots of one tree will rise out of the leaves of trees nearby.

Roots

ROOTS WORK DOWN into the soil, bending as they go, searching for the water and the minerals they need. They inch into the tight spots, bit by bit. They spiral as they travel, one way and another, as they grow.

The tips of roots are hard, with the growing parts of roots behind them, pushing. On the roots are tiny hairs that close around the particles of earth, pulling in whatever moisture they can find.

The roots of trees are sometimes much bigger even than the trees they lie beneath. Once trees have died the roots can stay beneath the ground for many years, hidden, sometimes long after we've forgotten that there used to be a tree.

They're underneath the ground, lost like sunken ships.

Butch

BUTCH is a stray cat, an orange male. As far as anyone knows, he's lived his whole life on the streets. As far as anyone knows.

A family who lives nearby once tried to tame him. They took him to a veterinarian to see that he was healthy. They paid for shots; these were to protect him from disease. They named him Butch for being tough enough to live outside.

Butch had an operation at the vet. The family had him neutered. This means he won't father kittens, and won't be as restless as male cats often are. Unneutered cats will wander, looking for a mate. They are anxious all cooped up. They have an urge to venture out into the world and leave offspring behind. As we do.

But Butch could not adjust to life inside. He'd taken up a habit of some cats. These cats will spray their urine on the walls. They spray this way to mark a place as theirs, to say "This place belongs to me."

In the end, the family let him go, although each day the little girl, named Leslie, would leave his breakfast on the porch.

The winters here are very long and cold – so cold that on the radio announcers say you shouldn't go outside. Your skin will freeze, they say, and so it can. They say to bring your cats and dogs inside.

Stray cats will often die on winter nights. They are not suited to survive such bitter cold. Their ancestors came here from warmer places in the world. The cat, as best we know, first lived in Egypt.

In winter, Butch would sometimes disappear. He would be gone for several days and then he would be back. There he'd be, making his way on careful paws across the crust of snow.

(When people came from overseas to make their home, no doubt they died of cold as well, like cats. They didn't have the heat and shelter we have now. They didn't have the skills to cope. And sometimes people with no homes still die in winter here.)

Four

Turpins' Yard

This happened in Halifax, Nova Scotia.

DAVID AND TIMOTHY COLE lived in a house next door to the Turpin family. The Turpins were English, and the English are famous for being good gardeners. The climate there is warm and the growing season long.

The Turpins' yard was beautiful and cared for – a mass of lush vegetables, drooping vines, great clumps of flowers, nodding sleepy trees.

The Coles' backyard, it was a yard and nothing more. Nothing grew. There was no grass. There were no flowers, no bushes; perhaps there were some tough and prickly weeds. It looked like any backyard looks when left without a gardener: just like a vacant lot. The boys would ride their bikes into the yard and spin out to a stop, raising dust on the hard dirt.

David and Timothy would stare at the Turpins' garden through the chain-link fence. They knew that it was beautiful.

One summer they decided that they would have a garden too. They started with lettuce. They bought seeds and buried them in the ground. They ran a piece of string around the place the seeds

24

were planted. They did this to protect whatever grew. They watered and they watched their garden carefully.

The lettuce never grew. Eventually, the winter came and went.

The next year, though, the seeds did sprout. They came up in the Turpins' yard. Somehow they had blown right through the fence and rooted in the Turpins' rich moist soil.

Annuals

SOME FLOWERS in the flower bed will die when frost comes in the fall. They'll die and leave their seeds behind to take their place. This is the course their lives are meant to take.

Other plants will die because they can't survive the cold. They came from warmer places, just like cats. To have these flowers we must replace them every year – buy them from the nursery, or plant their seeds ourselves in spring.

The plants that die in fall are known as annuals. This is a gardener's word. Annual means "every year."

Pansies are annuals. Petunias are annuals. Snapdragons and nasturtiums are annuals, at least in climates where winters get as cold as ours. They might not die in winter somewhere warm.

25

Perennials

THE FLOWERS that live through winter are perennials. Perennial means "everlasting" or "forever." These plants look like they've died when it gets cold. They drop onto the ground. They shrivel and turn brown.

But underground the roots are still alive. These plants will save their strength. They take cover from the cold. They'll come up through the ground next spring, most often even bigger than before. Perhaps in colder climates they'd be annuals.

Peonies are perennials. Daylilies are perennials. Black-eyed Susans are perennials and so are lilies of the valley, which grow beneath the maple, spreading further with each year, smelling sweet along the shady cobble path.

Five

Spenser

ONE SUMMER afternoon, there was
an unfamiliar sound above the garden.
It was a call – a loud and rasping cry.
It came again and then it came again.
At first there didn't seem to be an
animal attached. Nothing showed
its face among the leaves. And
then there was another call,
and then a flash of color.

By this time there
were human faces all
around the fence –
people from nearby
wondering what creature
might be making such a
sound, wondering if anything
was wrong.

27

In the tallest branches of the maple was a large pink bird. It looked something like a parrot, smaller than a cat. The bird was so high up that it was very hard to see. It seemed certain, though, that this was someone's pet. The bird must have escaped. This was not the sort of bird one normally sees here.

If you find a pet that's lost or seems to be abandoned, the thing to do is call the shelter — a place that takes in animals that stray. You call to find out if the animal you've found has been reported missing. But at the shelter, on that day, they said no one had called about a bird.

Outside in the garden, the neighbors scattered seeds and nuts, hoping they could tempt it to come down. This was not a bird that could survive a winter. The people in the neighborhood were worried for the bird.

The afternoon wore on. And on the telephone again, the people at the shelter said that no one had inquired about a bird.

Finally, in the garden, once the crowd had given up and gone away, the bird came down.

The bird stood in the garden, over by the fence: important, out of sorts, confused. Pink, with feathers fanning out above its head. Pink, with a predicament. Not someone to be taken lightly.

And then, the telephone — a man who'd had a phone call from the shelter. There had been a mix-up. He'd been calling up the shelter, leaving messages all morning. His messages had gone missing until now.

But things were straightened out. He said he thought the bird was his — his large pink bird, his cockatoo. It had escaped. It had flown out of his window in a high-rise at a busy downtown corner —Yonge and Bloor. He said he'd be right over.

Two young men arrived. The men were very handsome, well dressed. Two handsome matching males. They brought with them a carrier – a plastic case for pets, with breathing holes and a front door made of wire.

The man holding the carrier – the man who phoned – was overjoyed to see his missing pet. He called out, "Spenser!" He put the case on the ground, its front door open.

The encyclopedia says that cockatoos are indeed a sort of parrot – a parrot from Australia, a half a world away. They are intelligent – so say the books – and independent; don't like to be cooped up.

It seems, though, that Spenser was used to his new life. He waddled to the carrier. Not looking left or right, he stepped inside. The men got in a taxi with their bird and drove away.

The Maple Tree

MOST OF THE PLANTS we grow were brought from other places in the world – not these very plants, of course, but ancestors – that is, the plants they came from. In the past, explorers went on trips around the world to find new plants for gardens. They made such trips for centuries to bring these treasures home.

Tulips come from Turkey. Hyacinths come from Greece. Petunias were first brought here from Brazil.

The maple at the gate is a Norway maple, from Europe, across the ocean.

A garden, because the plants living in it come from all over the world, is like a zoo – a zoo for plants.

There used to be a real zoo – for animals – in the park across the street. This was when our parents and grandparents – our ancestors – were small. The zoo had polar bears taken from ice floes, and monkeys snatched from African trees. It had cages full of owls and jungle cats and tropical birds.

Where once there was a zoo across the street, there is now a farm to show the city children what pigs and cows and sheep are like.

But there are pictures of the zoo that once was there: the monkey cages – people looking in and monkeys looking out, both looking through the bars. The photographs are black-and-white. The women wear long skirts.

The government keeps these photographs at city hall. There are pictures of the city in the old days, of how it used to look, of how the streets looked then.

Next to the pictures of people who were powerful or rich, the names are written down. "This is a picture of Sir John Gibson." "This is the Honourable Harold Ferguson." They wear top hats. The names of children were usually not written down, nor were the names of people who were poor.

A picture of a mother and child on a broken Cabbagetown porch is titled "Slum Conditions." There she is, too thin, holding her baby in a backyard filled with dirt and boards. Their predicament is noted, not their names.

The maple at the gate was likely planted in those years.

The maple tree – the home to all the ants – by now was very old for such a tree. We know this from its size. It would have taken four or five small children, arms outstretched, to form a ring around the maple's trunk. These maples grow quite fast, for trees.

Plants keep growing all their lives. From their size we can often guess their age. Not so with animals – or not so, as a rule. Animals don't often grow in size once we've grown up. People, for example, grow smaller at the end if we grow old.

The Green Parrot

This story was told to me by a man named Graeme Gibson.

A MAN WHO went to Mexico brought home a bright green parrot. He brought it to Toronto, when the farm across the street was still a zoo.

The man had understood that parrots can be sociable, but this bird seemed indifferent – not very friendly, and the parrot didn't talk, as parrots are supposed to do. The man had children and a busy life. Eventually he decided he would find the bird another home. He took his parrot to the zoo and dropped him off.

The story would end here had not the parrot finally found its voice. As the man was leaving, he heard that voice behind him. The bird called out, as it had heard his children do, mimicking their voices: "Daddy. Daddy. Daddy."

When the little zoo was closed for good, the animals were taken to a big zoo out of town. The man went out to visit and he found a cage of birds. They all looked like the one he gave away. None of them seemed to know him.

Sometimes the children playing in the park across the street sound just like birds. While parrots on occasion sound like children, the children in the distance sound like crows.

A Bear in the Garden

WHEN SARAH MILROY was a child, she would play alone out in the garden in the afternoon. Her two sisters were older and they were off at school. Sarah would be put outside to take fresh air. It was a large green garden of sloping lawns and woods and neat but leafy trees. There was a golf course right next door.

One afternoon Sarah came to the back door. She told her mother she'd like to come inside. She said she'd seen a bear. It had climbed a little tree, she said. It was perched right at the top, swaying back and forth. It was a baby bear, but still too heavy for the tree.

Sarah's mother didn't believe the story. She thought her daughter had come up with a clever way to talk herself inside. Her mother said, "How wonderful! A bear! Offer him a cup of tea!"

That night there was a story on the news. There'd been a bear, that day, spotted on the golf course near their house. It had come down from the mountains. A baby bear, far from home. The experts guessed he'd come in search of food.

33

Seven

THE BLACK LOCUST • ON THE PATH AT NIGHT • TRESPASSER

The Black Locust

LATE AT NIGHT, in spring, the air takes on a scent — the perfume of a flower. The perfume is so strong and sweet it takes you by surprise. You look around and wonder what that lovely scent could be. It's strongest after dark, or just at dusk, when lights are going on inside the houses. This happens for a night or two each year.

If you follow from the garden, the scent will lead you down a cobble path. It will lead you through two gates to the park across the street.

At the entrance to the park stand two great trees, clumps of trees that rise into the sky, bordering the path that leads across the park and to the softball fields and riverbank beyond. The trees are big enough that children can climb up into the places where the trunks diverge, and in the daytime, children often do. The trees are old enough that boulders that were set nearby have grown into the trunks.

34

The tree expert who came to see the maple came across the street to take a look. He said: "These are black locust trees."

As spring comes to a close, the locust blooms with flowers. The flowers bloom in drooping clusters and send their rich sweet scent over the streets.

At night, when locust trees send out their strongest scent, the garden's quiet but it's not at rest. Plants grow most at night, when we're asleep.

On the Path at Night

OFTEN, late at night, you will see raccoons crossing streets downtown. Raccoons will suddenly appear, larger than you'd think they'd be, spotlit in the headlights of a car. They will suddenly be hurrying along, not looking left or right, pretending they don't see you.

Raccoons are quiet when they want to be. Even the biggest ones are able to move about the city without a sound. And sometimes they seem happy to make noise – at night, for instance, in the garbage cans. When they are fighting, you can hear them from a block away.

Raccoons get into fights high up in the trees over the garden. They send out screams so angry, from the maple and the mulberry, that lights go on inside the houses. People get up out of bed, cup their eyes against the windows, and look outside to see what might be wrong.

Sometimes you'll come into the garden late at night to see a little face in the

low branches on the path. The face is close enough to touch – bright eyes behind a mask, a little pointed snout. A baby, frozen like a statue, afraid, barely breathing, hoping you'll not see him, wanting you to pass.

The raccoon family would, no doubt, be somewhere quite close by, frightened for the baby, keeping still as well.

Trespasser

VERY LATE one night, a young man came into the garden. Not a child; old enough to be a danger if he wished. When he sensed he had been spotted, he suddenly stood still. He waited for a moment, and then he seemed to know he had been seen.

The man called out. His tone of voice was casual, offhand. He called out that this must be the wrong garden. He said he must have taken the wrong path. Just a mistake. He pretended he had not been trying to hide.

He stood a moment longer, then turned and went away. The gate opened, closed, and he was gone.

A trespasser is someone who visits, without asking, a place that you have marked off as your own.

Eight

FLOWERS • SEEDS • RUNNERS, BENDING BRANCHES, BULBS • TULIPS

Flowers

FLOWERS ARE a way that plants bring animals to visit. Flowers bloom to show that there is nectar to be taken. Nectar is a liquid sugar – a kind of food for tiny animals – hidden in the flowers.

Flowers lure all sorts of creatures: birds and insects, bats and human beings too. Think of how we follow, from the garden to the locust trees at night, follow their sweet scent. Think of how we stop to look at flower beds in bloom, of how we will buy flowers at the grocery store and bring them home.

When animals and insects visit flowers, they pick up pollen on their beaks and bodies and they carry pollen on to other flowers. The second plant will use the pollen from the first, if all goes well, to make a seed.

Seeds

SEEDS ARE little packages. Inside their outer shells are tiny plants, with a little bit of food to get them started, something like the lunch the girls took when they set out to cut the tree with scissors.

37

Plants have many different ways of sending off these seeds into the world. Dandelion seeds are blown away on bits of fluff. Maple seeds are sent off on propellers: maple keys. Seeds are sometimes hidden inside sticky burrs. They cling on to the coats of passing animals, and so are carried off. Animals eat seeds and leave them in their droppings, far away.

People carry seeds. We've carried them around the world. We carry seeds on purpose and without meaning to as well: in pockets and in shoe treads, on ships and in the holds on planes. They come with us when we travel, like pollen, like burrs on coats of squirrels.

Some plants send off their seeds by surrounding them with fruit. The fruit will tempt the animals to carry seeds away, as birds do when they make off with the mulberries, as we do when we come home with our groceries. These seeds we carry without meaning to.

Most seeds will never be new plants. The seeds must land where everything is right for them to sprout. Somehow they sense when things are right to grow – when the temperature is right; when there is moisture and the proper soil; when they're at the right depth in the ground. If conditions aren't just right, the seeds can wait. Some can wait a thousand years.

Runners, Bending Branches, Bulbs

SEEDS ARE one way plants make new plants, but there are others.

Some flowers, like the daffodil, grow up from bulbs down in the soil. Daffodils make new bulbs that grow beside the old.

Some plants can start a new plant from just a stem or leaf put in the ground. There are plants that send out runners – long shoots that grow out sideways underneath the surface of the soil. These runners send up new plants as they go.

There are trees and shrubs whose branches grow down low to touch the ground. Where they touch they send down roots to start a new plant in that place. In this way, one little tree can someday be a field of trees. In this way, there are plants that live for centuries, new parts coming to life before the older parts have died.

Tulips

This happened in spring about seventy years ago.

TWO LITTLE BOYS were passing time one day. They were wandering on streets of pretty houses – not their own streets, but not too far from home. As the afternoon wore on, the boys got thirsty. Instead of going home for drinks, they came up with a plan.

They came upon a house, a house whose path in front was bordered by a line of yellow tulips. They would pick the tulips, they decided, and they would sell them. They would use the money to buy themselves their drinks.

The boys pulled up the tulips and carried them, dirt still clinging to their bulbs, to the front door of a house. It was the very house, in fact, in front of which the flowers had been growing.

They knocked at the front door. A lady answered. The boys made their proposal. Would she be interested, they asked, in purchasing the flowers? The lady showed no sign at all she recognized the flowers, agreed to what they asked, and paid the boys.

Off they went to buy their drinks – chocolate sodas – a drink that children in the old days used to like.

The boys, of course, believed the lady hadn't recognized her flowers. They thought they had outsmarted her. If anyone was fooled it was the boys.

The next day, so they saw, the lady's plants had been replanted on the path. They realized she'd known the plants were hers.

How could they have predicted that the woman at the door would be so generous, so kind? The boys were young. They had a lot to learn about the world.

39

Nine

A House for Butch

FOR YEARS after the family let him go, Butch came and went among the gardens on his own, eating food the family still put out, sleeping where he could.

Sometimes he would be scraped or scratched about the head. At times he'd had to fight, it seems. He'd found a way to live, but life was hard. He didn't have a place to call his own.

And then one fall, a neighbor with a house close by took note of Butch's plight. By wintertime, before the snows began to fall, the problem had been solved.

The neighbor had a little house built at the hardware store. It was a wooden cube: two feet high, two feet deep, two feet across. It had a swinging door in front, a lid on top. Inside the house there was a bed of straw and fleece.

Butch understood, as soon as it arrived, the house was his – tucked into a woodpile, on a warm wall, on a covered porch. He moved right in the night the box appeared.

Butch's Visitors

ONCE SNOW BEGAN to fall, the year his house was built, Butch often stayed inside his shelter day and night. He would accept whatever treats you passed in through the door. There would be his face inside, orange, and not surprised to see you.

One morning, though, it wasn't Butch's face inside the box. It was another face, with smaller blacker eyes set close together – a black mask set behind a snout. A character we've met before. It was a raccoon. It had retreated, by mistake, to Butch's house at dawn. It was separated from its family, not at home. That morning when the raccoon family vanished from the garden, this one raccoon was somehow left behind.

It can't have been an easy day in Butch's house. Perhaps the raccoon didn't sleep at all, protected from the noisy human daytime by nothing but the little swinging door. When darkness came, it burst into the night. It crashed into the bushes. It was a big raccoon.

These days it isn't dark inside the little house. These days there is a lightbulb just inside the lid – a lightbulb set inside a wire cage. The lightbulb keeps the shelter warm and dry. It also keeps raccoons away. They want the dark to sleep.

But there were other visitors to come.

Another morning Butch began his day, not in his house, but sitting on the top. And in his house, it seems, there was another cat, a yellow cat, a stranger. The yellow cat had tags. He had a home, but liked to visit Butch's house as well. The yellow cat had somehow got the best of Butch. And so, down at the hardware store, they built a second house.

The yellow cat moved in and Butch took back his house. Both cats would take whatever treats you passed in through the door.

And then, one day, another cat appeared. This cat was dainty, brown and black – a kitten, really. A pretty cat with wispy fringy ears. And at the hardware store they built another house – a third.

There are now three houses tucked into the woodpile – three wooden houses with little beds inside of straw and fleece, with lightbulbs in the lids to keep them warm, and swinging doors and cats and no raccoons. There are blankets heaped up on the houses to keep the icy winds out of the cracks.

Sometimes a big black cat comes by. He has a wide head marked with thick white scars and ears that stick out sideways. He gets in lots of fights. He looks things over.

Three houses seem to be enough for now.

Winter

IN WINTER, in a garden, it looks as if the trees and shrubs have died. The leaves are off the branches. This is true of trees that are deciduous.

In wintertime we say the garden's "dormant," a word that means "asleep."

On the trees and bushes, the leaves and flowers are ready for the spring. They're there all through the winter, tiny, folded up, complete, and hidden in the buds. They've been there sometimes since the spring or summer past.

The plants will somehow sense when spring arrives and when their buds should swell and open up. They'll know it from the temperature and from the lengthening of days.

Spring comes early in the city. The human presence makes the city warm.

The Graveyard

BENEATH the mulberry tree there is an iron fence. The iron fence is square; each side is ten feet long. It's an old and fancy sort of iron-work.

Within the garden's fence, beneath the ground, there lie remains of raccoons, cats, and squirrels. Or so the story goes from families nearby.

People used to put these fences around the graves in graveyards to mark the places where their families lay. There is a graveyard near the park across the street, one of the oldest in the city. It contains some fences just like this.

Some people buried here were very rich, with little houses carved of stone above their graves. Others were so poor they didn't have a stone at all. Their names weren't written down.

There are people buried here who left their far-off homes to come to North America, but didn't last the trip. They died in shipwrecks, or of illnesses they contracted on the way. Their families, where they came from, might never have found out that they had died, would not know what became of them. There were no telephones. Some letters would arrive; some would be lost.

Some people who came here to live could not survive the change in their conditions; others did survive and put down roots.

45

Ten

Weeds

"STRAY" is the name we give to cats and dogs that don't belong to people. "Pest" is the name we give to creatures we don't want in the garden. "Weed" is the name we give to plants that grow against our will, the plants we hadn't meant to be there.

To "weed" a garden means to pull out unwanted plants when they are small enough to be pulled out. (Weeds come out most easily when the earth is damp.)

Certain weeds are frustrating to gardeners. They make their offspring quickly, or leave a lot of seeds. Some weeds grow back from tiny scraps the gardener has missed.

Trees of Heaven

THE TREE the raccoons climbed down in the morning – the tree at the edge of the flat-roofed garage – is called a tree of heaven.

Many gardeners call this tree a weed. There are several of these

46

trees here, on the edges of
this garden and in the yards
close by.

The tree is called a tree
of heaven because it grows so
quickly and so tall, as though
it's reaching up to heaven. The tree
has other names, some not as nice.

The tree of heaven first grew in far-off
China. It was taken off to Europe, where
it was grown on farms – grown to feed
the silkworms to make cloth. But the farms
could not contain these trees. The trees
sent out their seeds above the fences, and
out across the continent. Once in North
America, they did the same thing here.

The tree of heaven, it turns out, can live and
multiply in many sorts of soil. It can live
through dry spells and through hot spells.
It can put up with dirty city air. It can grow
in fields and vacant lots. It can come up
from tiny cracks in sidewalks and in garden
walls, on railway lines and roadsides.

This tree began to grow all over, in places
where we'd rather that it didn't – a trespasser
of sorts.

It's also called a stink tree. There is
a smell these plants sometimes
give off. A smell that we don't like.

47

And there are more complaints against this tree. Because it grows so quickly, its wood is soft and breaks. A wind will tear the smaller branches from the trunk. The tree of heaven loses twigs, and twigs must be raked up.

These days, the gardens on this block are weeded carefully. There was a time, though, when the gardens here weren't tended with an eye for how they looked. There was a time the people here were poor. Their worry was survival — food and shelter. They had more pressing problems than the beauty of their gardens.

The neighborhood was Cabbagetown, called this for the cabbages that people grew here in their yards. They used this land to grow their food.

It was back then the trees of heaven must have staked their claim.

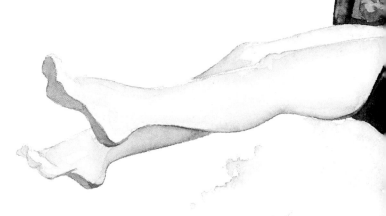

Eleven

Lizzie

This happened almost seventy years ago.

LIZZIE FELLOWES has a memory of swinging on a swing. She was very small – three or four years old. The swing was by a river, in her garden, in Quebec.

She remembers that the lilacs were in bloom around the swing. She remembers the purple of the lilacs going by. She remembers the purple of the lilacs going by, and green. The purple lilacs and the green of leaves, and the feel of the breeze and the smell of the water, and the sweet smell of the lilacs going by. The sound of the water. The smell of the lilacs. The purple and green. The sound and the smell of the river.

It's the first thing that Lizzie remembers: the joy of the feel of existence. The feeling of starting a life.

49

Twelve

The Second Tree Expert

THE ANTS continued their endeavors on the maple, circling and climbing on the trunk.

Another expert came to see the tree. He stood beneath it, quiet, for some time. He watched their busy progress up and down the trunk. He looked at the vast limbs above the garden, the wealth of tossing rustling leaves.

"The tree looks fine at first," he said, but then he pointed up to something no one else had seen. Partway up the tree were scraps of crumbled old cement, clinging to a hollow in the trunk. Someone, long ago, had tried to patch the tree trunk with cement.

"The tree looks fine at first," he said, "but don't be fooled by tossing rustling leaves. It's possible," he said, "the layers just inside the bark — the layers taking food and water up and down the trunk — are healthy. And so the leaves are green. It could be, though, the tree is weak inside. It's possible the tree looks fine," he said, "and still has hollow places in the trunk. The ants are living there and we don't know how big a home they've found. The tree could be too weak to stand up to a wind or heavy snow. Large pieces could break off, or it could fall."

50

He said that in the country, it sometimes is all right to leave a tree to fall down on its own. "A city tree should be cut down," he said. "A city tree could fall into a house. Someone could be hurt.

"This tree is very old," he said. "With winter coming on, I would suggest the tree be taken down."

Little Girl in a Tall Tree

This happened in the British Properties in West Vancouver.

MARJORIE HELEN, when she was small, went down the street one afternoon and climbed up into the branches of a tree. It was an evergreen. (Evergreens — just to explain — are trees that keep their leaves in winter, such as fir or pine or spruce.)

In Vancouver, where this took place, the temperatures are mild, the growing season long. Some evergreens grow tall. This tree was very tall, much taller than a house.

The evergreen that Marjorie climbed was just about a block away from home — next door to the Delman's house.

The Delmans were a father, mother, and a pair of pretty girls — twin girls, two peas in a pod. Mrs. Delman was pretty too.

Mrs. Delman had wanted to be a dancer when she was young, or so the story went. Sometimes she would dance in the living room to music from a record.

51

The neighborhood children would watch. She performed dances from the South Seas, twirling and knocking bamboo sticks together. The children said she might get a job someday dancing in a fancy Polynesian restaurant called Trader Vic's. She seemed like an exotic creature, a fancy creature, all cooped up.

But perched up in the tree outside her house was Marjorie that day.

Marjorie climbed up to the top, and then called out, proud of what she'd done. From her perch up in the leaves, Marjorie could see across the city, over bridges, past the university, and out over the ocean, whose waters stretch to faraway Japan.

As she looked over the city, admiring the view, a passing man looked up and saw her, and – very worried – ran off down the street to get some help. He knew this little girl and hurried off to find her parents. His instinct was, of course, to save this child from harm. He worried she might fall.

By the time her parents came, a little crowd had gathered at the tree. Her parents were both terrified to see their daughter up so high, but did their best to keep their voices calm. They worried that if she sensed they were afraid, that she'd be frightened too. She was too high for anyone to reach, up in the frailest, highest branches of the tree.

"Look at you!" they called. "How high you've climbed! Now why don't you come down?" On the ground the grown-ups wore false smiles and held their breath.

And down she came, cheerfully, carefully, branch by branch. Not slipping, not at all afraid, and safe. Marjorie had seen across the city, over bridges, past the university, and out to faraway Japan.

When Marjorie's father tells the story now, he says that it was he who found his daughter high up in the tree. He says she'd called to him by name: "Daddy. Daddy." And maybe that's what happened. It was too long ago to know for sure.

The Day the Tree Came Down

THE DAY the maple tree came down, two men arrived that morning. One of them climbed up high into the tree. He hoisted up a chain saw — a saw with a loud motor — and some ropes. He took off limbs and branches with the saw and, with the ropes, he lowered all the pieces to the ground.

The other man, below, cut the limbs to pieces. He stacked them up like firewood along the path. By lunchtime most of the tree was on the ground. The limbs were gone and just the trunk remained. It was a tall trunk left standing, much taller than the tallest man, but it was here the men were forced to finish for the day. It seems there was a problem. The trunk, you see, was hollow — more frail by far than anyone had guessed. It would indeed have fallen before long. But there was something else as well.

Looking up from down inside the trunk were faces, a host of gleaming eyes, set behind long snouts. It was the raccoon family. This hollow tree had been their home. The hollow part was large enough for all of them to live inside.

The men explained they had two choices. They could disturb the family – take a pole and push it in the hollow trunk and tease the family so they'd run away. Or they could put their tools away for now and go away themselves. The raccoons, they said, would move out on their own now that their home was open to the sky. Their shelter was destroyed.

And so the men packed up and left. They stayed away a week or two. When they came back, the raccoons had moved on.

The men cut down the trunk the day that they returned. And then another worker came and ground the stump out of the earth. She used a loud machine that gave off smoke and smelled of gas.

And this is how we found out why the raccoon family, who disappeared each dawn, had always seemed to vanish into air. We found out why we'd never seen them leave. The reason we now know: they never left. They'd climbed into the branches of the tree and dropped into an opening that none of us had even known was there.

I'll End These Stories Here

I'LL END THESE stories here. I'll end the book. But as these tales are true, they don't end here. We never know the end of stories in real life. We say there's a beginning and an end. We like to think we have the measure of the world. We like things to be tidy.

The truth is that our lives are lived within a story much too long to know. We only know the little bit we see. But books do end. And so, here are some bits to finish up.

About the raccoon family, truth be told, just mysteries remain. How long had they been here, living in the tree? We'll never know. Perhaps for generations of their lives. Perhaps for generations they were just inside the bark, right beside the path inside the tree. We passed close by beside them, inches from them, each and every day.

There they were as people came and went along the path, peering at the ants, sprinkling useless powder, pointing at the crumbled concrete, deciding if the maple should come down, talking loud, close by, not knowing they were there.

Where have the raccoons gone? We'll never know. They've moved their story off to somewhere else.

Butch, the outdoor cat, still sleeps inside his shelter on cold nights. The family who once took him in still feeds him every morning on their porch. His orange pelt hangs loosely on his bones. His coat is dull. He moves more slowly now and squints against the light on sunny days. These days he has a broad pink scar across his scalp.

Otherwise his days seem much the same; he goes about the business of stray cats. He goes about the business of survival. Leslie, the little girl, is almost grown. Soon she will be old enough to leave the nest.

As for the trees: someone noticed, just this year, up in the mulberry, metal cables stretched between the limbs. You have to tip your head right back and shade your eyes to see them. In summer they are hidden by the leaves. But someone once took steps, it seems, to give this tree support. The mulberry is old. It's likely that it's frailer than it looks. In all these years, no one had seen these cables.

And finally, there is another maple where the big tree was cut down — a little tree just yet, still straight and perfect. The twists and turns come later. For now it has a little head of perfect tossing leaves. No cables and no concrete and no ants. A Norway maple, delivered from the nursery to take the old one's place. By the time this tree gets big, most people who now live nearby will have died or moved along — moved their stories off to somewhere else.

And perhaps this will remind you of a moment you've encountered in this book: if this little maple hadn't been beside the gate where people come and go, no one would have noticed that a perfectly round hole has been dug beside the trunk into the roots. The hole is several inches wide and black as pitch inside. It goes straight down. It's very dark, and you can't tell how deep.

Recently, in spring, an expert gardener came to take a look – to see if it might harm the tree: this tunnel to the roots. She said: "It looks like something's living there. It could be a rat. A squirrel, perhaps. It's hard to say. Whatever's living there," she said, "it might be having babies. We mustn't fill the hole right now."

She's right, of course. Whatever's down that pitch-black hole should have the chance it needs to start its life. And chances are it will not hurt the tree.

"So, in the fall," the expert said, "I'll come and take another look. We'll see what has been living there. By fall," she said, "the babies will be up and out."

The End